GRASSHOPPERS IN THE FIELD

IN LOVING MEMORY OF MY GRANDPARENTS, THOMAS JEFFERSON FOSTER AND JENEVA FOSTER

Michael Shoemaker
EDITED BY: TAMARY SHOEMAKER

NEW HARBOR PRESS

RAPID CITY, SD

Grasshoppers in the Field / Michael Shoemaker. -- 1st ed.

ISBN 978-1-63357-448-9

CONTENTS

1   GRASSHOPPERS IN THE FIELD

In my mind I can be there in a moment
on my grandparents' farm
an escape from troubles and worry
lying in tall green sweet-smelling grass
azure sky above
cool damp ground beneath
hot thin stifling air
grasshoppers sail
up in different angles
going further than I can see
The buzzing of the insect world
surrounds me like an invading army
to which I pretend to surrender with half-closed eyes
The delicate moon far away translucent

When the grating voice and shrieking brakes
populate my crowded worldly space
you'll know where to find me
just in time for the spangled star rise.
You're invited too.
No notice, any time.
Just make sure to wipe your feet,
and don't slam the screen door.

2   MOONSHINE ON WATER

Between awake and asleep
I see a still sapphire lake
Smooth as glass
Silvery sheen
From moonshine
And mistiness
I cast off in a canoe
No owner or price
Floating from shore
Lying in the stern
Oneness with the lake
As if floating on the surface
Stillness and joy
Mixed like hydrogen and oxygen
Flowing beneath me.
Soft, simple, serene.

3   THY WORKS

Thy works are beyond
the tallest mountain peaks
lowest ocean trenches
densest planet cores
thinnest cloud layers
smallest microbial existence
largest galaxy superclusters
coldest snowmelt streams
hottest sun surfaces
sincerest thoughts
gentlest feelings
Selah

4   WHERE I BELONG

Latitudes north
draw me
where my destination
will be
a place
where I can
lean back in a camp chair
and breathe in the harmonious
smell of deciduousness
the red maple, white pine and sweet birch
and know from the heavens'
vaults and spires
down to the center of my core
in this late lazy afternoon daydream
that I belong
in thy enraptured arms
sheltered, courageous, warm,
bold and free
for today and tomorrow
until time's last
dangling moment of eternity

5   STARGAZING AT CAPITOL REEF

It's a mysterious nonmystery.
As I contemplate numberless
stars with the same mind
that counts out my correct change
at the checkout stand at the supermarket
I am baffled by the mathematical infinity,
An expanse of beauty I see
and yet I do not feel alone or distant.
There is something right on the outskirts
of the soul that lets me know
I am in some way more a beloved brother
than rejected outlander
to these living rotating masses of hydrogen and helium.
So glad you are here to hold my hand.

"Stargazing at Capitol Reef"

6   PA'S SECOND CHANCE

"But Jesus answered them, My Father worketh hitherto, and I work." (KJV John 5:17)

We all called Grandfather Foster "Pa."
With his wife and three children he left work as a mechanic
in an Arizona CCC work camp hearing the siren song promises
hopeful to find a good paying job in an airplane plant in
California.

The first week in town Pa went to the plant
there were 150 applicants for one job that day.
The men said it had been the same for weeks.
He prayed, "Father, what am I to do?"

Discouraged, nearly broke and desperate
on the second day and with a second chance
—he came once more
to sit on a cold cement floor and wait.

Then he saw 10 feet away a broom and a dustpan
and remembered years ago as a boy on the cotton farm
his father would rouse him at 4 a.m.
saying "Go to work, my boy. Go to work, my son."

Pa looked at the idle broom and dustpan
and heard again his father's firm, but gentle voice:
"Go to work, my boy. Go to work, my son."
Pa picked up the broom and started to sweep.

A plant official breezed quickly past Pa, then stopped abruptly
and asked, "Where is your security badge?"
Pa replied, "I don't have one because I do not have a job."
He waved, "Come to the hiring office and we'll get you a badge
to work."

Pa floated with finesse into the office like Fred Astaire
lifting Ginger Rogers effortlessly into pink billowing clouds
with the hope, promise and joy of a new summer's day.

So, when time is late and energy low
and I look across my desk with more work to go
sometimes I think I can hear,
"Go to work, my boy. Go to work, my son."
and return in the ebbing light
of an early drooping foggy winter's night,
"Yes, dear father, I go. I go."

7   FOUND UNDER MY FEET

Sitting at a picnic table
resting for a moment
I looked down and saw
teeming worlds
of red beetles
with black vertical bars
crisscrossing their territory
of a brittle maple leaf
leaving an autumn descant
of yellow, kelly and gold
showing its darkened
reticular spine
I spied two squirrels captivated
in a game of interwinding tag
prancing then pouncing in a whirl
up the pole of the nearest pine tree
the day ended with cascading canyon sunsets
and a brisk wind arose—so glad to breathe
deeply and take part in this parcel of earth
so oblivious to me

8 TAKING THE LONG WAY BACK

I trekked out
in a flurry
beating hot thin dust
on the trail
burdened with
the swiftness
of worry
and pretense.

On the way back
there will be
no such error.

I will take time
to lean on the
old picket fence
and stare at the
far distance of
the mist rising
above the hills
counting my brothers
the quail bolting
the trees
to lie on the
cool damp ground
in the meadow
tasting the tang

of wild raspberries
looking up
saluting the
bottom of daisies
listening to the musical
consonance of bees
that must also breathe in
the sweet smell
of the graciousness of grasses
to sit in playing
light and shadow
almost like a laugh
by the brook
with feet immersed
in cold brisk liquid—
self-transcendence.

You ask me
how to live,
this is how.

BACKYARD FROST

Frost caps my roses.
Didn't deadhead them, again.
Said I would, but never got to it.
No frost blankets protecting them.
The buds wear fuzzy frozen crystalline hats.

A mourning dove sits on a furnace vent
Hooting loudly to neighbors as
Steam rises in the air.

Frost envelops my grape vines.
Empty branches outlined in translucent ice.
Still, brown leaves clinging to part of the vine.
Crowding out images of delicious September harvest.

Frost disinterests our housecat.
Her face against the double pane window.
Stretching out her body to reach the last sun rays of warmth.
One paw dangles and droops from the windowsill onto the couch before sleep.

Backyard beauty links backyard beauty
Carrying a mantle of peace everywhere.

THIS AMAZING PIANO

When I am furious, I pound Beethoven
intense pressure and trembling fingers.
I am sorry afterward,
 truly sorry.

When I feel shy, I hide behind
mirthful Mozart or somber Wagner.
There is nothing out of place to
call undue attention.

When I am happy, my fingers
prance vivaciously to Gershwin
knowing there will be no parking tickets in my future
—almost honest, eminently hopeful.

When feeling amorous, I sail with Leonard Bernstein
soaring and sweeping sounds of sincerity levitating
higher than a butterfly, tree, mountaintop, moon
to scintillating starry sensations twinkling far-off.

In the darkest night, illuminated by only a piano lamp,
I play Beauty with awe and wonder at every touch,
so deep into the wellspring of the purpose of life
all I can do is feel, know, and feel afresh
too boundless even to raise water
 for one teardrop.

11   GEESE VS FLAMINGOS

It was not
    a pretty sight
        when Canadian geese landed
            in the flamingo enclosure
                at the aviary.
With honking
flailing thrusts of wings
wildly jerking heads and bills
storm of steps
speedily pushed, pressed
and corralled the fidgeting flamingos
to retreat into a murky pool of water.
The black swans with their cygnets
in the neighboring yard silently swam
to the farthest distance from the fray
imagining that staying away is the same as peace.
Even the cackling of the comic kookaburras
could not reset the ease of this auburn autumnal afternoon.
Tension was like buzzing oscillations of electric currents.
The flamingos emerged in deliberate defense, kicking
powerfully
but they made no damage, injury or advance.
Their salvation had to come from above.
The geese's attention flew to other blaring V-shaped fletches of
arrows

calling them in a light wind along with siren songs south to the
glassy horizon
and they trailed towards a removed sun, surf and serenity.

From a Borrowed Garden Palace

Vermillion violet
full fragrance
tumbles
from high trellises
over
    the
            wall
into a pool
casting
radiant resplendent
revolving kaleidoscope
reflections
dancing and darting
slivers of sunlight
completed in virtuoso
silen ce

flowers turn towards the sun
casting shadows
across the tall garden fence

    indefatigable marathoners
    sprint to break
    the finish line tape

        fighter pilot contrails
        crisscross the stratosphere

in a crosshatch pattern of white

loft, arch, lift, and serve
a tennis ball
over the taut net

lime-colored slithery seaweed
squelches underfoot;
searching for sun-bleached sand dollars

robin watches
me unearth
last year's beets

circling mist
bathe hanging moss
distilling peace

winter creek
congealing
wild ducks waddling

smoke stacks
shut down for good
breathe easy

river frog croaks
salamander slithers
while I doze

13   MELANCHOLY'S SONG

It's Friday and drizzling again
while you drive home
listening to the radio with me by your side
and the song comes on.

It's the one that sometimes thrills,
brings moods or something too hard to describe,
but somehow always
matches our souls.

You roll down the window to watch
tiny beads of water bounce off your skin
and just about everything smells as it was before—
something of lavender.

There used to be the taste of the sea breeze
on the tips of our tongues
and the warmth of our hearts
with tenderness and understanding.

You turn into my driveway, stop the engine and look at me.
Tears roll down our cheeks knowing what can no longer be
and what no longer needs to be said.
I get out of the car, shut the door and walk away.
The last note floats skyward beyond our reach.

14 NIGHTTIME NOSTALGIA

Rocking on the porch swing
wife out of town
couldn't sleep
wondering why she chose me
from a dozen or so
wasn't the strongest,
smartest, most handsome
still can't dance, write or
hardly speak to woo her,
but there's something
more like mist
smelling roses
hearing guitar
feeling rain
seeing sunrise
drinking well water
after working in the yard
taking a deep breath
—sparks and solace mixed
got to do better somehow
tomorrow for her
she's the one

15   BELONGINGNESS

When our eyes meet
sheer innocence
magnificence
tenderness
fearless
finds.

When our hands narrow
the space between canteros,
warm fingers interlace,
embrace
bliss.

When our lives entwine
thrilled hearts
and minds
flourish and fly.

Note: "canteros" in Spanish can be translated into English to
the word "flowerbeds."

16   WATERCOLOR AT 35,000 FEET

No snacks
water, no ice.
A child wets a brush
dips in orange
touches paper.
Color spreads fast and wide
an amazing creation.

"Look, Mom, I made a sun."
She gazes.
"I knew you would, sweetheart
—someday."

17   SPRING POPPY SUPERBLOOM

Granny counted turtles for the state of California
and was always good with numbers
a bookkeeping graduate of Pima Academy
in southeastern Arizona.

She would take me on visits to my Uncle George
through what I always thought was the Great California Desert
although I never knew the real name
being young enough that nobody expected me to know
anything.

One day on the drive, she pulled over the car.
We got out and Granny pointed to a hill.
"What do you see?" she asked.
Nervous that she would not like my answer,
I said, "Nothing, I mean dirt, no, nothing." She smiled.

At George's, I slept in the upper bunk in my cousin Cordy's
room.
I couldn't get to sleep with him wanting to talk and talk,
a country boy wanting to say something to a city visitor.
The rain pounded the metal roof all night, harder than I had
ever known.
It was enough for the desert to take back part of the road.

On the way back, Granny stopped and we faced the same hill.
Something new, a sea of California poppies, thousands—millions

a renewed promise after the flood of yellow-orange goodness
blanketed the hillside with simple majesty
that made my skin tingle.

I had heard of the Throne of God and thought
poppies must be the color of this Throne.

Granny asked once again, "What do you see?"
waiting for my answer, breathing in the desert life.
"I see heaven, just heaven, Granny, don't you?"
She smiled the biggest smile showing nearly all her teeth.

18 THE CORNER OF ONE'S EYE

There are many things you can see
out of the corner of the eye
although at times your brain denies
their existence and reality.

You may say that it's not looking
and that could be entirely true.
Indirect vision can be
useful in the extreme.

Seeing passing motorcycles on the left,
whizzing balls on the right,
whirling of wings and
twirling of batons can save injury.

When sitting with a child
no more vision periphery.
Central vision, listening ears,
feeling hearts, and you'll see.

HOLY SPACE

Not necessarily at Mecca
Egypt or Jerusalem
today's holy place
starts in my small room
where I kneel
in prayer and receive
the answer in my heart
of how to help
my brother
and go
directly to do it
converting any
and every place
into an ever-expanding
holy space.

20   A Quart Jar of Molasses

(based on a story my Grandfather Foster told me)

It was a nice warm day going home from school
I passed the Cluff ranch house by the creek.
Mrs. Cluff gave me a jar of molasses
I thanked her from my family for this treat.

Heading off again, I carried the jar
by the bottom for a few feet with one hand,
but cramps set in so I could not hold it.
I packed it with my things in one great band.

A quarter mile out, tired, with all to tote
I dropped my sweater, books, lunch bucket, coat and jar
on the dirt road with dust filming my throat
to regroup, regather, and organize.

I planned to wear my sweater and coat
picked up one and came the other, glued
sweater to shirt, shirt to arms, arms to hands,
hands to pants, pants to shoes in darkening goo.

What a mess, you can easily see, and trouble too.
I took the bottle of ooze, climbed through the fence
and hid it under a muddy bush, it's true,
cleaned all in the creek and hung clothes to dry by dawn.

A few days later, Mrs. Cluff saw Dad

asked him how he liked the molasses
"What molasses?" said Dad, looking had.
"The molasses I gave Tommie to take home."
"I never seen any molasses." This was no joke.
That night dad asked me at dinner, I almost choked.
I told him the jar was under a bush
not far from where she gave it to me.

Next day we went in the wagon
Dad had me point the molasses out.
Nine million ants liked it too, no doubt,
for that's where we found them, right near the spout.

Brushed off most of the ants in part victory
and took it home to a mother's glee.
She washed the jar off with soap and water
and we had hotcakes the very next morning.

Now you have seen into a poor boy's worried heart
over melting masses and of molasses
from a muddy morass and how it can start.

21   WEST UTAH DESERT

Crusted earth crunches beneath my feet
pulsating and throbbing heat
between the pale desert floor
and shimmering white sky
is a mirage which makes it appear
as if a purple mountain has risen
and levitates above the ground.
A light puff of dust from a distant gully
reminds me of the Pony Express riders
and that I am not the first to gaze on this openness,
a land of expanding wonders.
I find what I am searching.
Sublime quietness beyond comprehension, limitless clouds
and freedom reawakened and alive in me.

The late winter afternoon's advanced
slanted sun arrives
a half-spirited brother
to August's glowing orb
of molten heat
liquefying snow and ice sheets
dormant above the tree line
in mighty Elysian fields
where grey granite boulders
azured skies, pristine glacial lakes
and outstretched osprey talons reign

as congealed snow takes catalyst
from new spring's longer rays
aided by friction and gravity
water moves starting as a single
ring of a triangle to the powerful
tempestuous timpani and kettledrums
ending in a smashing crash of cymbals
in continuing creation's repeating
seasonal delight

weeks later
after heated hurried climb
feet immersed
between slippery silver stones
relieving swelling with numbing

cold water's cure
I sit astonished and in awe
heart swelling full with holy gratitude
that I too can be at home
in the canyon river's eternal abode

23 Zion's Continuous Standing Ovation

Scandalous, piercing Utah blue skies
             uphold surrounding and swirling red
bluffs in a light breeze
left in layers
          of sediment seas
               where blasted white
                    crustacean bones
                         and lifting red-tailed hawks
                              still testify
                         of millennia past
                    as this creek's frigid water
               runs over my ankles
and through toes
          spreading all loving whispered truths far downstream.
                         I bite most reverently
into a peanut butter and jelly sandwich, vowing
                    to never be the same
                         after this dangling,
          defining moment—of crystallized clarity—purified by
fallen tears.

Birds Alight

Diving first for a meal
Belted kingfishers alight in a blur
Waggling feathers and tails.
Mourning doves alight with wings whistling
Clearing space with a crystalline warning.
Noiselessly barn owls alight
With talons outstretched seizing hold.
Thousands of migrating sandhill cranes
Touch down flat in several steps.

TODAY'S WALK

We walk hand in hand in silence, contented within this touch.
Up the long driveway climbing and then around the corner.
Contrails from Hill Air Force Base draw quadrants
Against the background of a cobalt winter morning sky.

We rise to our turnaround conscious of time and demands.
You squeeze my hand in one motion and hold on firmly.
Of so many squeezes in our intimacy, which is this?
A reminder, a joke, an affirmation, calling my attention?

No, this squeeze raises warmth from my calves to my stomach to heart
And there it burns in the fiery furnace of blazing cariño para ti
After 29 years of marriage and further on.

26 THIRTY YEARS MORE WITH THEE

for my dearest Tamary

We walk today in symmetry,
down a path that leads to eternity.
With no trembling or anxious gait,
our fingers intertwined more of late.
More than a symbol of a bond
or conveniences that correspond.
Your love for me so radiates
fire's warmth that kindles then consecrates.
It's the simple things that ring so true,
before you leave for work, an "I love you."
At night you listen to my daily distress,
nodding, knowing me, just your presence a caress.
So, on next April twenty-three
while I clear my voice on bended knee
will you accept me knowing better the cost
for another thirty years though tempest tossed?

27   YOU AND ME

For me, to open the car door for you.
For you, to wear flowers in your hair.
For me, to wash my car before our date.
For you, to make me a picnic lunch.
For me, to feel special you made it for me.
For you, to blush when I thanked you for making it.
For me, to send you a love note.
For you, to call me on the phone
      and your crazy parrot to make
      a dog whistle because it recognized my voice.
For me, to dream of taking care of you someday.
For you, to rest your head on my shoulder while dreaming.
For me, to protect your life even before my own.
For us, to sacrifice our lives in happiness and love together.

28 THE MILKY WAY IS IN YOUR EYES

It's raining again.
Mary Elise, you are two years old.
I take a break from studying
and lift you with my left and strongest arm.
With the right, I open the sliding glass door.
As we pass on to the porch, the outside comes in and inside comes out.
We delight in the difference.

A racket made by raindrops pounds the roof.
You reach your pudgy hand out beyond the eaves
with the delicacy and grace of a black-necked swan.
You let your hand be moved by the raindrops,
turning your hand over and over again to a rhythm
and a melody of laughter that is all your own.

Another drop falls on your palm.
You look at it as if it were the first drop from creation.
You glance back and I catch for a moment in your eyes
something eternal, glistening with understanding, awe and glory that makes
me wonder and then believe that I saw a larger part of the universe that day because of you.

Books Transport

I look up at 6 p.m.
puzzled as to where
Saturday afternoon went
while the sun sets
in orange magical mistiness
hanging above trees
outside my back window
and the cat, Yuki,
slumbers near my feet.
I give a light sigh of satisfaction
glancing down in my lap
and seeing a half-opened book
with its bookmark idly holding
the place of the present
covering the next few words
of reading on the page that could easily
send me hurtling into the past
hiking my first summer in the Sierras with John Muir
arguing military strategy with Napoleon
crying with Victor Hugo
deliberating what would make the good society with Plato
shivering with Jack London
singing to all liberty with Walt Whitman
cooking with Julia Child
developing moral conscience with Charles Dickens, Harper Lee
and Gandhi

and building the Panama Canal with David McCullough
I toss the book onto the pile on the sofa
wondering why I am so hungry
and what might still be in the fridge to eat.
As I get up and go into the kitchen,
I hear prancing paws following in hopes to hear the opening of
a tuna can.

GRADUATION REACHED

I take a slow deep breath
seated and dressed in cap and gown
—clerical dress of the twelfth century.
No more sixteen-hour days
working a part-time job,
then class and homework.
No more group projects,
defending what I write,
or living on the testing knife's edge
between knowing and unknowing.
The field with rows of chairs
that stretch to infinity
is filled with the sweet scent
of freshly mowed lawn
unchanged
from when I sat here
as a new student at orientation.
I will miss the daily treasure hunt,
its rewards paid in doubloons
of partially dissipated doubts,
arising questions and aspirations.
Sitting here before others arrive
self-conscious, I say under my breath
to myself trembling with a smile,
"Good work, Mike, well done."

31 THE COST OF A HUMAN LIFE

I sat as an observer
in a state's superior court. First-degree murder was the charge.
Cold-blooded calculated murder was the act.
One teen on a sleepover was beaten to death
from behind with an aluminum baseball bat.
The teen pled guilty and the sentence
before final plea bargaining was two years.
The mourning wail of the dead teen's mother
rose far beyond the failing plastered court ceiling.
What is two years?
two visits to the CPA to pay taxes
twelve tire rotations
two World Series
four dental cleanings
two spring plantings
how long I have procrastinated
sweeping out the garage
twenty car washes
two work performance evaluations
for one human life.
I sat as a witness
in a state's superior court
as part of society
guilty.

32 AN ALARMING INDIFFERENCE

You call me your enemy,
but you do not know me.

my fears, mistakes, worries and woes
strengths, courage, and resolve.

You think we lap water from the same moving river
in the same way,
but you are mistaken.

Every winter will fall,
all piercing winds will bite,
bombs will continue to incinerate
our markets, streets, sanctuaries and sanity
until annihilation's scythe falls with its last blow.

Your grandchildren and my own will no longer
gather fragrant wildflowers in the fields.
You tell yourself
you have no need to know me.

Our loves are lofted away with the unsettled seeds of spring.
I am waiting as time closes its gates of possibilities.
Only peace makes us impregnable.
Seek to know me, forever.

33   Mountains in the Sky

Are the mountains
of the earth or the sky?
At sunrise, the mountains are
in silhouette from the light
radiating from above.
When you look at a mountain range,
do your eyes gravitate to the foothills or rise to the peaks?
In the afternoon, the clouds roll in as if they were the first in
existence
and roll over the mountain tops scattering light.
The lakes, ponds, and slow-moving streams
reflect the mountains, skies, and clouds.
Lightning strikes the ground,
but then quickly returns to the skies.
At night, the stars first appear and then multiply ten-fold,
a hundred-fold, and then beyond count or comprehension.
The Big Dipper and the North Star are never found
at the base of a mountain or by looking at shoelaces in the dark.
You must look up beyond the hills, trees, and nearly into
eternity.
Now whisper quietly your answer, are the mountains of the
earth or sky?
When I go to the mountains,
I am lifted up.

34 FLORIDA LAGOON AT NOON

Perspiration beading on my face
Finding a wrought iron bench
A temporary resting place
Under a magnolia
A shady space.

White-spotted eagle rays glide through the water.
Otherearthly, but ours, if we can keep them.
Using acoustic telemetry networks
Scientists listen to their shell crushing of clams
Hoping to learn how to help them survive.

Closing my eyes, the sounds of the lagoon seem amplified.
The slap of lapping water moving in and out,
The squeaky siren song of manatees,
The lusty rhythmic thump of the American bittern,
Lulls me to doze in the warmth and peace of the day.

GARDENER'S EXCHANGE

Half of all is not for me
In spring I grow
Spinach, beets, carrots
Radishes and lettuces
My soil grows
spring vegetables best.
Half is for the neighbors
Delivered in a bag

Half of all my neighbor's is not for him
In summer he grows
Squash, cucumbers, bell peppers,
Tomatoes and corn.
Glorious, beautiful and blessed
He delivers some to me

At summer's harvest my other neighbor knows it's not all for
him
All summer he grows
Roma tomatoes, jalapeños, green onion,
Cilantro, garlic and red onion.
My other neighbor combines these and other secret ingredients
To make triple hot tomato salsa
It is my favorite
It burns like an out-of-control fire in my stomach
Delivered in canning jars marked XXX in black permanent
marker

36   Man's Caving In

A new neighbor asked me,
"Should I plant a globe willow tree?
They seem to give good shade."
There should have been an easy answer.
But I saw the high-spirited look
in his glistening eyes, the "This is my first
and best-loved new homeowner idea."
I had seen it before.
Other neighbors planted willow trees
based on the decision they made before and
I couldn't warn them out of it.
This is the stark truth.
If you plant a globe willow
you will get good shade
from the summer heat in four years.
In ten years, the trunk will crack
due to the softness near the base.
In twelve years, it will die
and we'll hear the chatter of chainsaws again
and see one more dead willow tree stump
I can add to the three that I could
see from my porch that misty-eyed afternoon.
I paused,
then getting up, I patted my jeans, smiled and said,
"Where in your yard do you want the tree?"

El Significado de "Americano"

Me senté en el salón
de amigo Argentino
despues almuerzo
en un estupor
de somnolencia
en un calor agobiante

con los párpados colgando
no estaba listo
para la pregunta
de este criollo agudo.

"¿por qué ciudadanos
de los estados unidos
se llamen a sí mismos
'Americanos'?"

"soy Americano", dijo él.
"los guatemaltecos, chilenos,
y los bolivianos
son Americanos.
¿no, es así?"

empezaba a pensar
de una retorta traviesa
pero toda que salió
que es una tradición de

los estados unidos

tamborileando con mi dedo
en el brazo de mi silla y
pregunté, "somos hermanos, no?"
con sonrisa cariñoso
él respondió,

"sí, toda la humanidad
son hermanos, incluso
nosotros, hermanos
Americanos."

38 THE MEANING OF "AMERICAN"

Translated into English by Michael Shoemaker

I sat in the living room
of an Argentine friend
after lunch
in a stupor
of somnolence
in stifling heat

with hanging eyelids
I was not ready
for the question
from this sharp Creole.

"Why do citizens
of the United States
call themselves
'Americans'?"

"I am an American," he said.
"Guatemalans, Chileans
 and Bolivians
 are Americans.
 Is it not so?"

I started to think
of a mischievous reply
but all that came out

is that it is a tradition of
the United States

I drummed my fingers
on the arm of my chair and
asked "We are brothers, aren't we?"
With a caring smile
he responded,

"Yes, all of humanity
are brothers, including
us, American
brothers."

HARD WORDS

Hard words flew
in a second
through this room
they're not invisible
or painless
they're real
biting
pervasive
hurtful
powerful
I am so sorry
and would fly instantly
to heal
protect
repair
replace these words
with love and
a sanctuary of peace
but I can't fly
what words are left
in this empty space
except for a plea
to allow me
to try again

"A Restful Garden"

Purple and green
clover and violets
color in stone walls

the blue heron stands
regally—watching steam rise
above wetland grasses

First Lady of Song
Ella sings like sinking deep
in my easy chair

      an alligator
      lies in muddy ooze viewing
      birds with half-closed eyes

launch in heavy mist
current speeds, drops pelt, kids cry
excitement and fear

      chin up and beak raised
      head pivoting left and right
      throated chirruping

         casting light tackle
         high into the wind above
         crashing sounds of waves

narrow bills chirping
darting on spindly legs
bobbing for beetles

      javelins soar to
      impale the fluorescent sun
      then glide into grass

41   Mom's Maple Desk Chair

Sitting on the chair
she worked with
bills, taxes, mail,
pens, paper and pad.

In this smooth chair
varnished with care
her voice within
would hallow it with
silent prayers.

"Father, today, nothing for me,
all for them.
Please, keep my three boys safe
and let them always feel Thy lasting grace."

I never heard these silent prayers,
but know them as well as scripture memorized.
Looking past her glasses and through her eyes
I see the words in her heart,
the wellspring of love that never dies.

MY UNCLE GEORGE

When I look at the American flag
I think of Uncle George.
He served in the U.S. Navy
during the Cuban Missile Crisis
did fleet training at Guantanamo Bay.
Quiet, unassuming, almost always with
a gentle smile, Uncle George,
an American hero.

When I look at the field of blue
I think of justice done.
Uncle George gave twenty years
to the Atlanta Police Department
went through riots, bomb scares,
drug busts and shootouts.
When swimming with his son and nephew
he had to explain two long scars
on his stomach from a knife fight.
Blue-eyed, mustached,
an American defender.

When I see those stars
I think of purity of heart.
Listening so closely to even
hear Uncle George's voice
when he said grace over the food
because it seemed to him

that the only person who needed
to hear his thanks was his Father.
A praying American believer.

Tears drop as I look at the stripes
and think of the valor of spirit and how
Uncle George battled with colon cancer
for two years never winning always losing
against the ravaging tsunami of pain then rested
his head for the last time
with his wife and daughter looking on,
my American fighter.

43   Zion Canyon's Song

Contrails lance sky
mauve mountain peaks
descending mists kiss
copper riverbed roiling sands
thunderclaps reply

FROM THE LAST PEW

Not feeling worthy
to approach any altar
I slip in unobserved,
but by Thee

Dear Father,
hear my cry
forgive my sin
give Mercy,
mercy,
one
more
time.

My heart lifts
like a dove
released
from a cage
with Power's
freedom flurry
through morning
light's window
rising upward,
heavenward
secured by
Thy love.

45   BE JUBILANT MY FEET

My feet lean into this incomplete puzzle path of life
to Wisconsin to visit my eldest daughter
to the store to pick up the gallon of milk
I promised yesterday to get but forgot again
to visit the Ozark Mountains to photograph our avian friends
and the hospital to hold a hand in commingled pain and relief
My feet go anywhere, everywhere, for any reason
led by Jesus Christ.

My feet guide me on Sunday to witness,
behold Jesus's precious bleeding feet
from nails dripping purity and love
these feet, these feet wet with my tears
Oh, be swift, my soul, to answer Him!
Yea, Lord, I will go with Thee always!
Glory! Glory! Hallelujah!

VALLEY OF NEEDS

While elite philosophers
from mountain tops
waste away and bicker
over the existential meaning
of glistening mirrors
of lakes and seas
send me into the valley
to serve my neighbor.

A man
struggled to find
the remaining sleeve
for his arm
while putting on
his coat.

Unseen I lifted
from behind
his coat sleeve
was on
and he was off.

Left behind
my poor heart
changed
innocent and clean
send me,

oh, send me
again
into the valley
of multitudinous needs.

"Did Not Our Hearts Burn Within Us?" (Luke 24:32 KJV)

47

When I was sick
and opened my eyes
and you were there
consistently caring for me.
When I was down
and you came
and shared
the Word of God
gentle as the
morning dew on
the purple foxglove.
When I was out
of money
and you gave me
a meal freely.
When I was weak,
ashamed, worried
and sick of a host of sins
and you encouraged me
courageously.
When it was so dark
that I could not see
and you lovingly
and carefully led me
by your hand

to His Everlasting Light.
Did not our heart
burn within us?
It still does.

AN ORGAN FOR THE CENTURIES

Spreckels Organ Pavilion, Balboa Park, San Diego, California

In 1915, the Austin Organ Company built the Spreckels
Organ and Pavilion and John and Adolph Spreckels gave
the organ and pavilion to the City of San Diego. The City
of San Diego provides 52 free to the public Sunday con-
certs a year, and maintains the instrument and the Civic
Organist position with the support of the Spreckels Organ
Society. 109 years of playing music and still going strong.
https://www.spreckelsorgan.org/
President Woodrow Wilson pushed a telegraph button in
Washington, D.C.
to open the Panama–California Exposition by turning on
the power and lights at Balboa Park at midnight December 31st,
1914.
This new park supported native wildflowers, bobcats, rattle-
snakes, and coyotes.
The expo celebrated the bifurcation of North and South America
by the Machine Age magnificence of the Panama Canal
and to show the progress and possibility of the human race.
The First World War broke out in Europe that year.
The Ford Model T was the most sold car.
Most people ate Red Flannel Hash—corned beef hash
putting in extra vegetables.
It still felt like a new century, still a new beginning.

organist sweeps

falling leaves from keys
while lifting chords

hurricane force
pipe organ winds
thrill my soul

organ pedal practice
deeper than running
in grape vineyard sand

when Bach's brilliance
opens the bellows,
who can close them?

49 PARENTS, BE CAREFUL WHERE YOU LET YOUR CHILDREN PLAY.

A small girl of six
At the Sunday concert sits
next to her baby brother
on the lawn pulling
the tops of blades of grass
delicately, deliberately
putting them into her other hand
creating a green mound of mush
that she dumps on her brother's
head until he starts to cry.

Parents, be careful where you let your children play.
They may become the next Civic Organist of San Diego
to play the world's largest outdoor musical instrument.

Hotel Roberts

Provo, Utah

Wisteria wilt in an open vase
The sands of time lean forward
leaving silt
blocking all motion.

Hotel Roberts found room enough
for a missionary training center
and gave shelter from
transients to presidents.

Once a National Historic Place
then razed due to water and structural damage,
what remains?

Honeymoons, anniversaries, birthday party bliss
sultry summer nights of business trip boredom
doors slamming, someone asking for another glass of water,
a word, touch, recognition, smile and warm embrace
still throb and pound the ground with a lively heartbeat
at 192 South University Avenue.

51 FROM A HIGH SOUTHERN UTAH PLATEAU

I shift my feet in the orange dust,
widening my stance and shading my eyes.
What can I see within a hundred miles
looking south from Zion's?

I see my ancestors in the 1860s near Grafton, Utah
called by a prophet,
planting orchards, farming, digging ditches and praying
asking "Have mercy on us, O Lord" and they found mercy.

I see a mother of the Anasazi Tribe holding her child
close to her heart
on the banks of the Virgin River near the evening
where the orange sun pours into a pool beyond the horizon.

Rio Grande Depot

There is a chain-link fence
around the old train depot
caging possibility in
human connection out
living a dried up
tumbleweed existence
with no roots
or place to roll
millions of atoms
held by strong attractions
the potential energy that can
convert to kinetic energy
through mechanical work
bringing cataclysmic change
now.

53   I Am a Bransonite

On my visit to Branson, Missouri,
You decided to gently feather sunrise
in sublime golden gleaming splendor,
light dancing on the tips of treetops
pouring by measure with relief
into a worried soul and tired heart,
emptiness evaporated by Your touch.
I felt and knew it, as a witness.

Joy to the world, the Lord is come!
Let Earth receive her king!
Forty-one years of Christmas family performances
with drums, electric piano, guitars, video and lights
an addendum to two hundred and seventy-one years
since written, with millions of voices and attending angels
lifting praises to starry skies over shepherds' fields.
I see, feel and know, as a witness.

One man, one woman, an acoustic guitar.
Two voices singing, two hearts beating as one,
fingers interlaced, holding hands,
eyes filled, love effulgent, everlasting, evident
married decades ago, before God in holy union
surrounded now by children and grandchildren—
air, light, peace, laughter, truth combining the eternities.
I will go from this place, witnessing on my way
it is this sweet Jesus who blesses me every day.

54 CREAM PUFF, LE MAGNIFIQUE

You say that you put vanilla pudding in a cream puff?
I thought this was a misdemeanor or a felony.

Oh, cream puff, what is it about you?
With the first bite, I instantly hear
the first eight measures of Debussy's
Clair de Lune, not from a piano,
but the orchestra's string section.
Doesn't everyone?

Your pillow of puff is your golden crown
and below is a white cream
that could blind the whiteness
of the brightest clouds on a summer's day.
To eat you is like breathing blissfulness.

And so, you see
my roommate fair
I am justified
hucking that tennis ball at you
down the hall
when you made off with
—the last cream puff—so stealthily.

ANTI-POETICAL SAYINGS

You will have to pardon me
in these times of trouble, inflation and sleaze
for rattling off a few anti-poetic sayings
with astonishing rapidity and ease.

"Preparing munchies for the lunchies
while restless at breakfast" is a classic
saying you really cannot doubt,
but "catching sneezes in my sleevsas"
is another you can tout.

You can "toil and moil with cooking oil"
morning, noon or night
or "middle for diddle" aiming for
the great bull's eye of life.

So, to poets with a modernistic flair
when you're tired, weary or worn
feel free to join the bandwagon spree
of anti-poetical sayings long forlorn.

You'll find it something magical
To lessen the mind's pollution breeze
if you endure with patience
this gentle little tease.

BUNSEN BURNER BLUES

You seem to think that I can
turn on and off my liking for you
like a blue-flame Bunsen burner
in a high school chemistry class.

Hydrochloric acid can burn
through my best pair of jeans,
but it can't burn through
what my real feelings for you mean.

I know what you've been saying
and it may be halfway true;
you claim it is only a rotten case
of the Bunsen burner blues.

Once we were chemistry partners,
but you're now so far away.
Whenever we go to the movies
you won't even let me pay.

Oh yeah, I can feel it deep from my head to my feet
a bad case of Bunsen burner blues, playing on repeat.

It gets so cold and lonely in the chem lab late at night
the squeaky wheels of the janitor's garbage can give me quite
a fright.

Chicken noodle soup cooked over the burner for one just won't
do.
What do you expect from me, to ring out a cock-a-doodle-do?

Please say that you'll bring me back and I will be such a gent.
I'll wash out every beaker, measure attentively each experiment
and even pay back what I owe you
every single last cent.

Until you make your decision and we can reignite,
I'll be singing the Bunsen burner blues, it's true,
morning, noon and night.

Oh yeah, I've got it bad, the Bunsen burner blues
for you.

57 ARTIFICIAL INTELLIGENCE IS COMING

You may call it paranoia,
but it may be a real-annoy-ya
when you know that AI
is coming for you.

They say, AI, you will
replace 5% of
white-collar worker jobs
by 2030.

If you want my notion,
and if it would be no trouble
you can take my job with your magic potion
and I will feel like I won a daily double
with Ken Jennings on Jeopardy.

AI, you can take my doctor,
dentist, accountant and replace
them with machinery,
but careful with my barber
who I need so desperately.

You can take all the legal beagles
content marketers, paralegals
and you will hear no remorse,
but cheering from the cheap seats
until I am hoarse—indefinitely.

And so does it really matter
if I never have to parallel park
or write a letter ever again?
Come and get me, AI,
I am ready. Let's begin.

When I Sleep, I Do Not Dream

58

I do not dream when I sleep
and this is where
elucidations begin.

Specialists say everyone dreams,
but some when they awake
forget them.

Cousin Cordy says I have always
been on the weird side.
To this, I have no reply.

My friend shrugs her shoulders
and says she wishes
she could buy a cheap
non-dreaming plan,
to bundle with her
wireless and cell phone.

My boss asks if I need
to see someone
(anyone other than he)
in that caring-befuddled
half-listening, concerned face
sort of.

My wife shrugs her shoulders.

My golf buddy says there are worse things
and marches on to tell me five.
My cat does her meow-yawn...

and this is when I decide that
when I sleep and do not dream
on the inky side of my eyelids
it is just all right with me
to daydream an afternoon away.

59 THE WAITIN' SEA

Poets spend 98.7% of their time
in the waitin' sea.
Submit a poem to a journal or anthology,
a manuscript to a publisher,
an application for a residency,
a poem to a prize contest,
and it bobs and floats weightlessly
in the endless waitin' sea.
Do not interpret this as glee in me

to sing out a brassy sea chanty
but while I sit in the doldrums of the waitin' sea
just watch me go on a shopping spree
buying 14 colors of socks for a manatee
installing a disco ball in the dining room
in the summer house in Capri
and sitting on the deck to see
the paint dry on
my friend's used Maserati
an expression of humble humanity.

Yep, checked my email, again today.
No response that I can see.
I sent it 11 months ago optimistically.
Perhaps the editor is translating it
into a dead and forgotten language
meticulously.

And then...and then...it comes so effortlessly.

Hello Michael,

hope you are well, thank you so much for trusting us again! We will be back soon with a date to publish your poetry.

60   RED LIGHT, GREEN LIGHT

People drive cars all night and day
and need to follow rules
to find their safe way.

At a place where two roads cross
and there is a traffic light
a green light means
the driver can go
and a red light means stop.

When drivers follow this simple rule,
all can cross the street without being hurt
including my friends and me
and my best friend's dog, Burt.

SOME LIKE IT THIS WAY, SOME DO NOT

61

My brother likes to spread peanut butter and jelly
on separate pieces of bread
and then squish them together to make a sandwich.
I have no idea what is going through his head.

Not me!
I like to mix peanut butter, jelly and honey
in a bowl that makes a gooey glop
and then watch it fall from the spoon
onto my bread in one big plop.

We both have our different ways,
it's very plain to see.
They both have their place.
How glad I am we can choose
due to God's Good Grace.

NEWSPAPER BOY

Mid once upon a time
and just a day ago
I still breathe the stiff smell of newsprint
while sitting with my father, mother, brother
in our living room placing ad inserts
rolling hundreds of papers and swiftly sliding
them into their smooth plastic sleeves.
The long word "responsibility"
awakening me at 4 a.m.
to lift two equally weighted carriers
onto my bicycle handlebars.

I emerge from our garage with tense calves
straining and pumping
pumping and straining
with rhythmic squeaking
leaning forward on the vinyl banana seat
into the outer space of fluorescent streetlights
and the thumping of my tires over squares of sidewalk.
By 5:30 a.m. I return triumphantly done with the route
zooming with a weightless feeling into the carport.

Why did I work a paper route at 9 years old?
The money did not hurt, but it was never enough.
For Nancy, my next-door neighbor
who wanted to know if it would rain in three days
to know if her rheumatism would be kicking up

for Henry, down the next block
waiting to scour the want ads
always looking for his next best job
for Patrice, across the street
who read the gardening section
to find out how to get the weeds
out of her front lawn
and earwigs off her strawberries
for all the obituary readers
(and you know who you are)
to sift among truth, myth and the fantastic
lastly, for me, being needed and needing it
—the desire for warmth of conscience
for the dignity of work and service.
While I never said I loved this job
many still catch this moonbeam in a bottle
even working from morning to night
every day.

Out of the Sand Trap

By no means
should it work
but it does
almost every time.
I close my eyes tight
hardening my grip and
swing in one wishful
chopping motion.
I open my eyes
to rowdy cheering
in my head
with the ball
resting on the fairway
just five yards from the pin
as sweetly as a baby dozing
put down for an afternoon nap.

Tennis Team Yearbook Photo

Tennis action photo shots are angles,
all elbows and non-tanned knobby knees
no cool golf strokes smooth and glossy,
but much better than the wrestlers
sweating profusely on the mat
intertwined in something awkward
that looks much more
than a pretzel brotherhood pic.

Was I happy then?
Did I know only happiness as a title
such as coach, friend, principal or parent?
It is not. For happiness is a
choppy jungle whitewater rafting trip
that really ends with blinding white Gulf Coast sand
llamado el fin del camino—lleno de fe.

65   ANOTHER MILITARY COUP

Shallow breathing - high piercing sirens screech in the streets -
crouching shoulders - whispers -
fences keeping enemies of the state in - keeping the will of the people out -
curfew enforced - four checkpoints to cross the city -
barricades - identification and documents key everywhere -
demonstrations of force by authorities to threaten underground resistance -
- an injury here - a disappearance there -
no assembly of groups over six people - the pounding of a door -
entrance without warrant - yanking of an old man from his bed of slumber - furrowed brows -
food lines - scarcity -
mother covering the mouth of her crying baby to not call attention -
puppet polling stations - secret police -
 false accusations of neighbors for safety - betrayal -
the stench of burning books and uncollected trash -
no electricity - all Internet down - suspicion -
one shot -
 entering a fleeing young man's arching back - he crumples on the sidewalk in
a pool of his own blood -
a warning to all of us - the spirit and fight for liberty continues.

Global freedom declined for the 17th consecutive year.
New coups and other attempts to undermine representative government destabilized Burkina Faso, Tunisia, Peru, and Brazil. Previous years' coups and ongoing repression continued to diminish basic liberties in Guinea and constrain those in Turkey, Myanmar, and Thailand, among others. - Freedom House, October 2023, https://freedomhouse.org/report/freedom-world/2023/marking-50-years

My City Walk

It is time.
I push the freezing metal bar to open the door
and find myself in a different scene.
From subdued fluorescent lights, carpet, warm forced air and
cubes for people,
to the great bold and white world
I move without reservation or hesitation.

Brightness
is reflected from melted snow on the pavement.
Brightness
from the sun gleams through the clouds.
In between snow glides and so do I.

A corner to the right and then to the left
and I am already gone.
My security name badge clipped to my belt means little now
because even with the name
I am part of the great sea of anonymity.

The walk signal chirps as I move smoothly across.
Still outside I take a right halfway through the block
and step on stones that came from Israel to the Salt Lake Public
Library Square.
Each stone makes the sound that a rock makes when it shifts
under your feet while crossing a stream.

I cut across the square with stones without looking back because I know the way.
steel grey bank of clouds
three lightning bolts hit the ground
three-hour delay

between clothes baskets
crouching low, leaning forward
ready to ambush

stoneware, pottery
flint, soil, free your tale of
one hundred seventeen

billowing tall clouds
rumble across the valley
cold drops pelt my skin

rhythmic pumping of
arms, legs, arching back rising
to dizzying heights

all in the stiff wind
lift to vaulted heights with ease
then dip and dive down

I would, but not for
could be possible, or not
maybe, but not yet

rain plops on leaves of
gold, auburn, and orange mixing
a soggy delight

man steps around man on sidewalk
to watch opera
about suffering

"Blue Lake at Sunrise"

ALL IN A POT

One November late afternoon
    slanted shadows
        fell on white sidewalks
            on a dead-end street.

My missionary companion and I
in Córdoba, Argentina
pressed our bicycle hand brakes
seeing something we had never
seen before.

A man was stirring
something in a huge pot over a wood stove.

I asked him, "What is this?"
Without looking up, he replied, "A pot."

I asked, "What's it for?"
Not looking up and with a dragging
tiredness he said, "Comida, Comida."
"For food, for food."

Not wanting to bother him
and appreciating his economy of words
we withdrew our bikes to the curb
to watch a scene unfold.

A young girl skipped by
handing the man
a softball-sized white onion.
Chop, chop, chop and in the stew.

Young and old came
with lima beans, diced tomatoes, radishes,
beets, carrots, peas, squash, potatoes
and a butcher found some ends of beef.

All who gave one thing
returned and partook
of what seemed to be new.

Laughing, clinking of glasses, guitars and singing
waft with the wind through open verandas
while all who used to be only one were now all filled together.

DRY LIGHTNING ON AN ARGENTINE PLAIN

The lightning runs its destructive course
not to pig, cattle, or horse,
but to the field with the farmer standing by
thunder clouds completely dry.
Spark is set, blaze ignites.
Fire grows to reach towering heights
leaving nothing of wheat kernel or stalk.
The farmer falls to his knees in shock
left trembling like a leaf in the wind.

PASSING CUSTOMS AT THE
BUENOS AIRES AIRPORT IN THE
'80s

Customs officers weren't supposed to take passengers' possessions for their own.
They did so unapologetically but always with a courteous smile.
The fourth person in front of me
made his donation of a new Rolex sports watch.
A woman teared up weeping silently, teeth chattering,
when they confiscated her gold bracelet
a gift from a granddaughter.
To me, they dropped my most precious possession
a second-hand camera, back into my luggage
with a worthless muffled thud.
Even the pat down into personal places made me wonder
if the soap when I shower needs to make it a little further in the future.
Then there were their questions filtered through my active movie-goer imagination.
I had seen the cinematic evidence where if you answered a question wrong you were silently swooshed away and eventually your bones ended up in the bricks of the new courthouse, palacio de justicia.
So, when the customs officer asked, "What is your purpose in Argentina?"
I would have fainted except for spying my friend Mario's hand-waving
a Lone Ranger across the white plains of linoleum oblivion,

at last, I knew I was safe.

INFLATION CAN KILL

Desolation guided desperation
with a silken cord to destruction.
Córdoba, Argentina,
    1989
        monthly inflation
         194%
Grocers put no prices on goods.
They knew while people shopped
the worth of what was in their
baskets evaporated into thin air
as if by one stroke of a
maniacal magician's wand.
Shopkeepers closed their stores
and locked their doors which had
iron bars on the windows.
Food could not be bought at any price.
My missionary companion and I stayed alive
because of one gentle giant of a man
who would open his kiosco en la casa
local shop in his home
under the dead of night so we could buy food
and stuff as much of it as we could into backpacks
and quietly carry it away on bicycles with wheels
that creaked so loud down empty dark city streets.

One day, my missionary companion and I saw
from a bluff overlooking the city

a group of a hundred people or so
from all walks of life heading somewhere.
I asked a man I trusted what they were doing.
He smashed his used-up cigarette nonchalantly
under his boot and said that they were going
to loot that store, pointing his finger north.
I asked what will happen if the police try
to stop them. He shrugged,
but the three of us knew the ticking final answer,
the cold hard math.

71   POCITOS, ARGENTINA

In a place known as "little holes"
less in value than Nazareth
two missionaries taught
far from home,
but not as far
as when Jesus taught
being His Father's
Only Begotten Son
condescending to earth.

Polvo, polvo lands, lies, lifts again
nestled in the nostrils of dogs
and men de bebida fuerte
lying face down on hard clay
at noon breathing lightly
in Pocitos Central square.

Bicycles, bicycles, missionary wheels spinning
fast as falcons descending and angels in flight
rain forecast, but one family waited
enough, enough to ride on dirt roads
fourteen miles out and fourteen back.

Missionaries sit, family members stand, as dark clouds gather,
turned over twin paint buckets, the only seats they own,
phrases burst from Spirit's fount
"Faith, repentance, baptism,

freedom, freedom from sin and death,
through God's only Begotten Son
who gave His life for us."
All that heard agreed to baptism.

Missionaries rode, so full of beaming, redeeming joy,
rain on the road was drips and drops, cracks and rivulets for
ten miles
then stream, creek, knee-deep deluge with wheels stuck in
muddied muck
three feet deep and three miles to go.

Against the purpled sunset
two bicycle crossbars
raised high to carrying shoulders
bruised, but not broken
drops of tears, sweat, pain, agony,
love effulgent.

I will always remember Another, Holy is His Name,
who bled great drops of blood
from every precious pore
for me.

Note: "polvo" is translated into English as "dust" and "bebida
fuerte" is translated as "hard drink."

72   GRATITUDE FOR THE ABSENCE

"Offer unto God thanksgiving; and pay thy vows unto the
most High" (Psalm 50:14 KJV)

Thank you today
for the absence
of what came before.

leave from yelling
release from taunts
rest from envy
stilling of disputes
comfort in loneliness
relief from poverty
emancipation from sin
delivery from ignorance
curing of illness and injury
relief of worry
answers to prayers

Some surmise
these changes are
impossible in
one lifetime.
Millions attest
nothing is impossible
with God.
He loves to liberate the captive;

we rejoice in redemption.

73 MY SUBSTITUTE WARRIOR

At the end of the news hour
they noted your death
in Afghanistan
and I pondered...
Just that morning
I cinched up the laces
of my hiking boots.
Just that morning
you cinched up the laces
of your US-issued army boots
for the last time
and last sacrifice.
I am no relation.
The only tangent
where we cross
is that you were from
Temecula, California
and in high school
I once ran a cross-country meet
in Temecula.
Through this silent media memorial
I find you are my age.
To my brother and surrogate
thank you for gifting me life
to see the light in my
unborn son's eyes,

for time to teach
my daughter to ride a bike
and to see
my thirtieth anniversary.
It may not seem worth the cost,
but it is everything and more to me.

ALMOST EVERYTHING IS UNSEEN

Middle school students visit a local university
to see a scanning electron microscope
for the first time.

"Can you see that?" asks the cell biologist.
Several 11-year-olds shrug their shoulders
and others declare nothing is there.

The technician prepares samples for viewing.
What was not there is magnified a thousand times.
A 3-D image like a round bathroom sponge appears.

"What is it?" asks one of the students.
"It is something you walk on every day, soil bacteria."
In awe, the students peer at the tiniest universe they can see.

The scientist unveils other samples of a moth egg, amoeba,
barnyard grass and wool fiber, previously the mundane,
but now somehow more striking, magnified.

"When you could not see with your eyes what is before you now,
did they not exist?
Did they only begin to exist when you saw them by microscope?"
questions the expert.
A resounding echo of "no" bounces off the shiny white lab floor.

"Some say you can only believe what you see with your eyes.
Is this true?" asks the prober.

Time rests as if each is holding their breath under water.

Then a student at the end of the row blurts out,
"What a minute! If you can only believe what you see with your eyes
that means you would hardly believe anything because almost everything is unseen."

The examiner blinks, closes his eyes and nods.

SHADOW AND SHIMMER

You say we are through
and no doubt,
we are.

It was so hard
to see when
the sun shines
vertical above us
at noon.

But as the sun slants
to the west
I view it more clearly
in your brass-flat
answers and questions
what I told myself
and denied
would ever be.

I never wanted
our continuance
to fall into the shadow
surrendering treetop to leaf,
bark to the insect-filled forest floor,
but it did, and here we are
left still as friends.

In our plain embrace
surface stream's dance delivers—shimmers
light's last leaf's lingering luster
twirling ever on water
going, going, so long
and gone.

Stopping to rest near frozen trees
huffing deep, visible breath
through winter's web
of white's crystallization
the blood pulsing
through my sore calves
on this senseless, sunless
morning sojourn.

I realize for one quaking, truthful moment
 sours my stomach,
 she's gone
 it will not change
 there's no going back.

Steaming tears drop
to my hiking boots.
Through soft fur
my hand fumbles for faith
around the corners
of my dog's pointy ears,
feeling for a future that
will be okay, somehow okay.

I fear the growing hoarfrost in my heart.
Help me, oh, please help me, dear Lord!
His aid comes with the gentleness and stillness

of silver snowflakes.

He is my Rescue and Refuge. Amen.

SILVER LINING

It was clear
Betty May loved Leon.
He was good to her,
didn't raise his voice
and treated her with respect
that she knew she deserved.

Leon's father owned a pizzeria
where he worked 10-hour days.
Betty May loved Leon and pizza.
He had a stable job and
she would not go hungry.
Easy math—she married him.

Leon died fifty-eight years later
almost as quietly as he lived.
She thought she would never
speak, sleep or eat again,
but her lighthouse clock in the living room
ticked on and so did Betty May.

In a parking lot weeks later
she honked her horn at me
and rolled down the window of a new silver car.
She asked, "You know what I call it?"
Not waiting, she said, "It's my silver lining."
Then drove away, smiling to herself.

"AND HE FRANKLY FORGAVE THEM BOTH" (LUKE 7:42 KJV)

Jesus answered a Pharisee
of two different debtors
one of five hundred pence
another of fifty.

Though different debtors the same
for both had nothing to pay
to free themselves from their
equal mountains of unpaid debt.

Not one penny could either pay.
It could have been one penny
or a million, impossible for both.
In my miserable sin, I sit and see
the math of infinite mercy in that
He frankly forgave them both.

Though years ago in Capernaum taught
words come to my mind and heart clear as the first
bold break of the sun over the mountains
"My son, I forgive you all, you are free."

79 "I Saw Thee Under the Fig Tree" (John 1:50 KJV)

Unconvinced by Phillip
Nathaniel asks if anything
good can come from Galilee.
Phillip replies:
Come and see.
Jesus identifies him as an
Israelite with no guile.
Nathaniel asks:
Whence knowest thou me?
Jesus says, "When thou wast
under the fig tree, I saw thee."

No fig trees in my town.
Jesus, from where knowest me?
From the hospital, just before surgery
when I couldn't stop shaking due to fear
at the laundromat washing my clothes
talking with family on the laptop
on the ladder painting my house
washing the car for my first date
trying to soothe our sick cat
pulling weeds in the backyard
the nights I could not sleep
you saw and calmed me
like a storm on an unbridled sea.
With Nathaniel, I say,
"Rabbi, thou art the Son of God;

thou art the King of Israel."

80 "The World Is Gone After Him" (John 12:19 KJV)

Of Pharisees
many viewed
few heard
and none were
recorded disciples
of Jesus Christ,
but they feared
the world had
gone after him.

Disciples
ran to the tomb
climbed a tree
rose from the dead
touched His garment
walked on water
were tortured and killed
—all to follow Him—
and us?

SHE STRIVES

On her own
she sets up
for her boy's birthday party
hanging streamers
preparing presents
tying tinsel
rolling paper for tables
setting chairs in place
paper plates and bowls
cups and place cards
balloons for everyone.
They come in chaos and cacophony
eat, run, romp and go leaving the cleanup
for the honored uninvited guest.
Mother sweeps, mops, takes out the trash
to the dumpster in freezing rain
and then heads home.

That night bone tired
from being up since six
getting her other children
off to school
she rocks her baby boy
in their existence of two
held in the curve of her arm
a secured sacrifice,
sublime sleep.

Out of Panama

Petrels softly lifted in the updraft
then in an instant splashing for food
then resting as if nesting on a swell.
In the distance
a white line above the horizon
then almost imperceptible
a black mass
suggesting something not of water, but land.
Pink transport ships
pull most of their cargo
immersed in green liquid
nearly the same color of the trees
that surround us.
Wind from cruising at 20 knots
cutting waves with a roar.
I am the least needed part
to keep this system moving,
but receive much from being present
in this bottle of marine delight
cast off to sea.

Clouds Over Southern Mexico (in English)

What variety of clouds that delights.
A cloud whose bottom appears to be drawn with a straight edge
to the horizon and the grey sea.
Another cloud that is so large that it consumes all of my visual
panoramas.
It is lofty and grey with white highlights.
An additional cloud that billows and is like a piece of popcorn.
Clouds, I take joy from your beauty.

Nubes Sobre el Sur de México (in Spanish), translated by Michael Shoemaker

Qué variedad de nubes para gran alegría.
La nube más bajo aparece dibujado con un borde recto
un horizonte y el mar gris.
Otro nube tan grande que consume todo mi panorama visual.
Es elevado y gris con reflejos blancos.
La nube adicional que se hincha como un pedazo de la palomita
de maíz.
Nubes, tomo gozo en tu belleza.

WITH FAITH IN THEE (IN ENGLISH)

84

We breathe to sing praises,
move to rise from our beds,
see to paint the heavens,
cry to understand one another,
laugh to fill the world with holiness,
smell to know the magnificence of magnolia flowers in spring,
write to remember Thy gift of tongues,
run to do Thy will,
and when we can't do any of these anymore
our hopes still reside in Thee.

Con Fe en Ti (in Spanish), translated by Michael Shoemaker

Respiramos a cantar loores,
movemos a levantar de camas,
vemos a pintar los cielos,
lloremos a entender uno al otro,
reímos a llenar el mundo con santidad,
olemos a saber el esplendor de magnolias en la primavera,
escribimos a recordar de Tu don de lenguas,
corremos a hacer Tu voluntad,
y cuando no podemos hacer ninguno de esos más
nuestras esperanzas todavía moren en Ti.

85 No Digo lo que Tengo en Mente

Mis pensamientos son mios
que no se puede dudar.
Con quien compartirlos
depende en quien puedo confiar.

Mis experiencias me dice
hay personas engañosos y
mentirosos con intencíon
a dañar.

Pero mi corazon es mío
y si sigo que veo, eschucho y siento
por medio el espíritu Santo
puedo actuar en mas confianza y fe.

Aun no soy perfecto
y hago un montón de errores.
Dios me dado este don y
sé mejor en quien puedo confiar.

Poetry when done right
is more than a cure
a greater find
than Newton's fallen apple
a higher opus
than Gershwin's "Rhapsody in Blue"
being eternity's sure arrow
that sends me straight to you

87 PRIDE IS A LONELY STATION

When pride arrives
people depart
leaving nothing warm
or lasting.

Who pride invades
thoughts slice inward
as a surgeon's scalpel.

Where pride resides
it oozes through cracks
pulling apart relations

Who pride rules
is left alone
listening to a fading
horn in the distant
inky dark.

INDECISION

There and here
near and far
thoughts scatter
like dry leaves
in an updraft
lofting higher
than this
apartment complex
and a compromise
is made to delay
making a decision
and play pretend
that nothing
consequential
happened today.

Barber's Advice

I am mum when any barber
gathers scissors, electric razor
and especially a straight razor
to shave closely the back of my neck.

She starts, "Yes, I once knew
a man who his doctor told him
to take some pills. He didn't,
then he died."

I would nod, but she already
leveled my head by putting
it between her two hands
with a slight shake.

"I once knew a man who
his doctor told him to
go in for a surgery. He didn't,
then he died."

Sweat rolls profusely down
around my ears dropping
flat on the tile floor.

"I once knew a man who
his doctor told him to go to
physical therapy. He didn't,

really too bad, he died."

I thank her, cough and tip big.
As I leave the shop, a text comes in.
"Are you going to make it
to your doctor's appointment
next Wednesday at 2?"
My reply is
"Yes, of course."

90 YES, LET'S TALK OF REALITY

Rhinestone stars
black felt heavens
opal illuminated moon
silver-sequined seashores
only in my dreams
are less real than
parking tickets, dog catchers, treachery,
desperate destruction
       and doom
snuffed out
with a thumb
and forefinger
along the candle tip
of all existence
by my memory
of your
simple glowing
deed of deliberate
kindness
today

You are the apple
of my eye, but sweet juice comes
from pineapples too

      Double-check the count
      of stars, I will keep my first

sum—infinity

Absorbent cotton
bath towels drip water in pools
soaking my poor feet

     I mow the lawn
     enter and watch the walls inside
     till I mow again

Why do I have to
splash through mud, muck and grime while
leaving the car wash?

a glass, cup and bowl
can all help to hold back
a flood in the desert

free drink, hot dog and keychain
to buy
a forty-thousand-dollar car

     an umbrella to wet Portlanders
     —a stick used to point
     out tourists

          beachgoers need
          winter outerwear
          when wind whips at fifty degrees

roaring, riveting
pouring, penetrating
cascading thunder
crash course rain
bride's veil
salmon seeking
moss-a-making
dripping drippy drip drips, Can I count this as four? No, only
one?
rockeroder
leaky ledges
hiker's refresh
squirreltopia
ice cycle staircase
sunshine rainbowsifter
snowmelt sink
pebble spreader
taki-more tumbling
deer oasis
tadpole playground
flightless fluid feathers
mountain deluge
river's mother
leaf diving board
stone slipperfier
dew's envy

troll toe dip
flashflood fury
mist escalator
breeze's lavish robe
a glass of water, please, twenty more to go
swollen-foot soaker
flat hair moisturizer
green's watering can
sunsets serenader
churning cauldron
lily pad lounge
nature's spray bottle
mold incubator
hikers' anklesprainer
twig's cannonball jump
ice climber pick hold
bubbly brew
crazy kayaker's course
drizzles' downspout
stone crusher
snapabranch
post-glacier galloping
slough-a-snow
climbers' crutchbuilder
sanitysalve descending

THE ROAD TO BEYOND

Shading my eyes
from blazing sun
I gaze as far
as I can see
and just beyond
mercurial safety
no guarantees
mystery
yet, I go on
with valor

93   AUTUMN ORANGE

I'll whisper to you a secret.
Spring beguiles, summer struts
and winter whistles away.
I am more at home with autumn orange
in its simple charming splendor.

Orange in the morning sunrise
that almost surrenders before it begins
and trees' leaves ablaze in color sweeping
down mountain slopes with the wind.

Orange in the feeling of plentitude
taking one's time on aimless walks,
raking the leaves half-heartedly and
lingering longer in others' words.

Autumn orange, once more cradle me
in timelessness, safety, tranquility.

RENEWAL THROUGH FRIENDSHIP

You come to visit
with a smile, "hi"
and "how are you?"
Promising to stay
only a minute or two.

You listen to my stories
of cats and bills,
bad arches and spills,
car repairs and dentists,
and growing grandbaby thrills.

You share a "remember when"
with a laugh and your same smile.
Then you stand and apologize for the time you have spent
as if you were an inconvenience and not heaven-sent.

Our moment together lives within me for an hour, a day, or week,
and gives me the energy, determination, and courage I seek,
to face this old stone world.
Thank you, my dear friend
for sticking through it with me to the very end.

FALL FLOWERS

Bedazzled by colors ablaze
and the lilting sway of dancing
autumn falling leaves
flowers can be forgotten.

Salvia, snapdragons, sneezeweeds
coneflowers, crocus, chrysanthemums
verbena, dahlias, strawflowers
—a leitmotiv of lyrical loveliness.

I am forgotten while waiting,
crossing a street, riding on a bus,
melding me like street chalk
after an unforeseen thunderstorm.

Fall flowers sing a crescendoing melody
that carries worth and meaning
to my small space in the universe.

SUMMER YELLOW

Bouncing tennis balls
wide brim straw hats
roses climbing trellises
picking summer squash

lemonade with crushed ice
in tall thin glasses
broad shade umbrellas
construction flaggers' vests

dripping melted butter
off corn on the cob
reading a book at the library
about a man with a big yellow hat

marigolds, begonias, petunias, daisies,
sundresses, beach balls, flip-flops, nail polish,
garden gloves, swimsuits, popsicles, golf balls
meadowlarks, warblers, goldfinch, tanagers

glow-in-the-dark shoelaces that show up
while eating popcorn in a cool dark movie theater
sunflowers reaching through my neighbor's
chain-link fence into my backyard

turning yellow autumn leaves rustle on my porch
convert to brown mid-rain, snow, and slush

dreaming in my chair in the winter dark
summer yellow returns

with a blazing noonday sun in a cornfield
growing stalks twelve feet high

Floating back and forth
swinging in the swirling stream
sweet sounds in the leaves
like the flight of piccolos
flickering above the flutes.

A brother at bat,
one pitching the tennis ball
me in the outfield
a hit over my head which
the dog shags and dashes home.

Brazilian blue bliss
from hot savannah rise these
squealing screechers then
land so near me peering through
whited eye rings warily.

WINTER QUIETNESS

Winter could have been conspicuous
showy or ostentatious
if not for its timorous silence.
No rustling of dry leaves
as a deer approaches.
The babbling brook is bound
in congealed ice.
No exasperating droning of
neighborhood lawnmowers.
Not a bumble bee buzz,
as I sit in my front porch chair
drumming nearly noiselessly
with my fingers in warm woolen mittens.
It seems as if winter has given up on sound
and I am consoled that all that is left is
the tender tinkling of wind chimes
over frosted frozen fields.

98 Pioneer Cemetery Cleanup

She told a lone granddaughter, just above a breath
with raspy broken tones, there was no longer
family enough to tend the garden of granite
and watch the violets wave in the grass.

She wept, until limp
—a sorrow-soaked blanket.

The granddaughter went to their church leader
in hushed hesitancy, sharing the family's woe and hope
for someone to care for the graves of those who crossed
blistering prairies to lush wide-open Oregon fields.

He promised to visit the site and speak to others.
It was as described, a sea of billowing bracken,
faltering fence, and grave markers, nearly
a complete check on nature's evergreen list of recapture.

They came, not one, but many, not for a month, bringing
with them a mower, shovels, hats, hoes, rakes, smiles, faith and
laughter.
Most were 12- or 13-year-olds who would tell their descendants
how they found Jesus, bended low on hands and knees
carving away weeds from stone.

While heavy dew descends,
landing luminous liviana in her lap

she sits to watch the next generation tend,
heaven-struck, once again and forever,
"Thank God, oh, thank you, dear God."

Note: In Spanish, liviana translates as light.

LAMPPOSTS IN THE PARK

Friends in Christ
are lampposts
in the park
gleaming in rain
glowing through fog
penetrating the sleet
guiding my steps
over uneven pavement
radiating all through
the night
leaving warmth, glory
praise, and joy in a
disciple's secure
peaceful embrace.

"WITH THE GLORY WHICH
100 I HAD WITH THEE BEFORE"
(JOHN 17:5 KJV)

Jesus submitted to be born
in an imperfect world
and asked
for the glory He had before.

He submitted to walk the roads of Galilee to heal the sick
teach the words of life and freedom
suffering mocking, beatings, scoffs and a crown of plaited
thorns
and asked for the glory He had before.

Isaiah taught Lucifer's ambition,
"I will ascend above the heights of the clouds;
I will be like the most High,"
for glory like the Father or more.

Jesus submitted bleeding from every pore
giving His life on the cross meekly
and asked
for the glory He had before,

But He will come again in
"clouds of heaven with power and great glory."

Dear Father,
I do not know much about glory.

Help me to make it through this life
and when I die may I please come
and dwell with Thee in everlasting
love and peace?

"And He Did Cast Himself into the Sea" (John 21:7 KJV)

Dear Brother Peter
after denying Jesus thrice
you could have felt all was lost
except your Master is the one
who rejoices in finding
lost sheep, a piece of silver
and the prodigal son,
being the merciful Christ of all new beginnings
calling you without hesitation
to find His sheep and even His most vulnerable,
His lambs.

Let me be with you, Brother Peter
casting myself without pause into the sea
and swimming my stroke by thy stroke to the shore.
Others must come in the little ship
to bring in the catch of one hundred fifty-three
but let me not hesitate to plunge, plunge without
fear into the Sea of Galilee.

I am good to swim the three hundred feet.
Let me share your burden straining all
to bring in the miraculous catch
dear Brother Peter
and then leave you and your fellow disciples

to dine with your Lord basking in His Light
while I slip away not ready for this meeting with Jesus
and go to visit the sick, imprisoned, the unwanted.

Someday, Brother Peter, we will meet again
and I promise I will be ready then.
Please, wait for me.

102 EARTHEN VESSELS (2 CORINTHIANS 4:6–7 KJV)

Earthen vessels are we
containing the excellency
of His power
not of us.

Smooth, not cracked or broken
no outward appearance
that anyone should desire
these vessels of faith in Jesus Christ.

The enemies of our souls
raise us high and cast us down
to crash on the floor, laughing
—giddy for our annihilation.

And yet, we roll intact
along the floor
smooth, not cracked or broken
to tears of evil designs frustrated.

What is the mystery of our protection?
Tempered in daily afflictions as hot as
King Nebuchadnezzar's fire for our brothers
Shadrach, Meshach, and Abednego
we are defended and delivered
by the Great God of Israel
and Him alone we will serve,

smooth, not cracked or broken.

healthy greenery
creeps down the throat ending with
a slithering gag

grace, poise, small steps first
swinging arms behind, knee drive
spring, splash, elation

grey swells lift and fall
waves surge, crest, crash and carry
us to sun-bleached sands

dandelion seeds spray skyward
like snowflakes rising on the breeze
to red rock plateaus

no more in shadow
afternoon snow thaw
drips in a steady stream

hoarfrost-covered trees stand
as soldiers' silhouettes
against frosted frozen waterfalls

black crows launch skyward
pine needles spiral down
upon our heads

my droplets cascade
into a bubbling brew
water, soap and knives

ingenious hidalgo Don Quixote
pirouettes near, not piercing
windmills of imagination

beachgoers need
winter outerwear
when wind whips at fifty degrees

a puff on my cheek
from a desert dust devil
enlivens me to heat's white line
rising on the horizon
reaching for a far-off gliding hawk

looking back
the train moves
out of sight
with me craning to see
lost dreams on the caboose

Like a formidable train barreling out of a tunnel in a billowing blur directly at you,
you hear the somehow controlled and practiced dispatch
"Take everything with you. Your services are no longer needed."
Not even one word for each of the twenty years of
service—sterile-efficient-economical.

A security guard escorts you out while you carry heavy frozen
productivity in a cardboard box.
What do they think a 54-year-old man is going to do,
stab someone with scissors that were always too blunt to open
a bag of Cheetos?
Your body goes limp as you push fingers through your hair and
tears drop
 —too early for any final whistle and too late for the sinking
knife of reality.

What will you tell your wife?
Sitting in the driver's seat of panic, desperation and a vocation-
al disappearing act, you mutter
"I'll think of something, must think of something."

ON THE CURB

Father, I am on this curb
with no place to go.
I thought I was strong,
now I know that I'm weak.
I was healthy,
but now I am sick, cold,
lonely, desperate—so tired.
Father, you provide for
the birds of the sky
and the fish of the sea,
will you help? Please help.
Somebody comes up
and gives me a blanket and
directions for a place to stay.
One of countless prayers answered.

OUT, OUT

Out, thou enemy of my soul!
No longer will I listen to
your dangling pernicious words of hate,
persuading whispers of sedition,
or laughter at my misery.

In me, you will not find a safe harbor or shelter
from the brightest beating sun of truth.
Reprobate of heart, mind, might, will and reason,
I am not neutral and will not yield or run.

I will stand with the Son of God,
my Defense and Shield in all peril.
All your aims for me will fail and fall forever away.
I choose One—the Man of Gethsemane
who bought me with His blood.
Victory, victory for one day.

CHALK FLOWER POWER

Snow in the mountains
Rain in the valley
COVID-19 pandemic
The gym is closed
Will walk outside
Pull on my hoodie
Walk out the door
Head over to school
Walk under the eaves
To avoid getting wet
Dry under the eaves
Wet everywhere else
Cold and miserable
Walking back and forth
Like a caged tiger
Ready to pounce
Wait, what is this?
Under the eaves
In a corner
Of the front
Of the school
And a wall
On the cement
Is a chalk flower
Lavender-white petals
Green-white stems

A marvelous mirage
Almost raising from the pavement
Full of fragrance
The young artist left stubs
Of different colored chalk
Everywhere as if in a rush
After the recess bell rang
The artist gives a gift
30 Utahns died from
COVID-19 today
Fear strikes
Uncertainty swirls
Worry stalks my door
But, with one chalk flower
One vision
There is hope and vitality
To the point that
I can feel the grass
Between my toes
Sprinkler water all
Over my body
And the warmth
Of the sun on my back
Sweet momentary relief.

RAG RUG

An unpresuming genesis
cull tired out t-shirts
or sheets that will never again
greet in the deep keep of slumber

slit with scissors, hold on tight
while a grandchild in destruction's delight
rips two-inch fabric strips
roaring and racing across the room

take three strips together
loop the ends together
braid hand over hand under
forming a masterpiece of finger momentum

start coiling this sinuous serpent
sew off the end, overlap, and beginning again
cut the last three strips
taper, sew, and tuck to hide the end

Why do some believe the only way
to get the dust of creation out of a rug
is to beat it relentlessly against
the brutal bark of a tree?

Shale rocks on an incline can be a problem.
My brother and his friends with longer legs
sped and scurried down the west side of the mount's face
bushwhacking the trail in leaps and bounds
with calculated slides to reach
the cars (waiting to take us home) with gleaming windows
in the receding afternoon sun.

Shale rocks on an incline can be a worry.
Burdened with a fifty-pound pack and hiking boots
two sizes too big, I first lost sight of the rest of the group,
then lost all sound leading me to stop and bend over
to catch my breath, heaving in the smell of pine trees
in the presence of no other human being.

Shale rocks on an incline can be dangerous.
Desperate, behind and afraid,
I too cut the trail and jumped, tired and timid,
down, down into a shale rock field a hundred feet long
until I was stuck—petrified.
To try to ascend meant I'd slide back in place
and to try to descend would be
uncontrollable destructive momentum.

My fears foresaw me clearly as a lonely
broken crumpled motionless mass
at the bottom of a ledge on a switchback of the trail.

Shale rocks on an incline can have a purpose.
Still not being able to move, I did what Mom taught
and prayed to know what to do.
The answer came in a clear voice, "Drop and roll."
I quivered in my determination but dropped
into a ball and rolled my best roll.
My body rolled at a fast, but controlled pace
for three-fourths of the field and
I landed on the trail below with a puff
of white dust looking like a ghost
without a scratch.

With time to kneel, I prayed to offer God my thanks,
then in young new liveliness started to run
to the desert floor where the cars were waiting
 with their high beams illuminated.

ALL IN A BOX

Topiary is the horticultural practice of training perennial plants by clipping the foliage and twigs of trees, shrubs and subshrubs to develop and maintain clearly defined shapes whether geometric or fanciful. —Wikipedia

From my resort to the asphalt parking lot there are,
count them: one, two, three, four, five, six, seven
carefully cultured, severely shaved, subshrubs as
square as Amazon boxes forming security,
predictability and manageability in this orbic world.

From surrounding Zion's oval living room there are,
count them: twenty-one peaks or high places from
which comes a choral eruption or revolt in
Gregorian chant only partially dampened by the
Virgin River's translucent spring sloughed off snow
now running wild.

Twenty-one messengers singing,
Seven boxed-up shrubs.
I like the odds.

And yet...there are boxed-shaped cars, checking off boxes at a doctor's visit, bento boxes, cubicles and offices shaped like boxes, cajas con forma de mochilas, cajas de plástico para leche, box shaped paid reserved parking structures, opera boxes, luxury boxes or suites at sporting events, treadmills where the only safe place to put your feet is in a box, voting in boxes to fill in boxes, eating out of Kentucky Fried Chicken boxes, gift boxes, returning Red Box movies, urban condo boxes and even eco-friendly raised garden boxes. No wonder that slow travel is the fastest-growing travel trend in 2024. I read it somewhere in a lit-up electronic box.

Twenty-one to seven.
It seems we should be
winning a little bit more.

MOPPING AT LEISURE

Simple, casual, barefoot
relaxed, rhythmic
rocking in
rocking out
pushing in
pushing out
like sending
a friend on
a playground swing
higher than school top
following swallows
into mist and clouds
daydreamy laconic
almost Sleepy Hollow
where even
soapy bubbles
on their own
elevate me from
this frigid frozen
wasteland kingdom
of northern November frigidity
and dumps me direct non-stop
into white sand and sun sensation
dangling my foot
over the beach chair
etching earnestly

what I deem as art
with my big left toe

Then...BANG! ... the mop drops.

FROM THE BOW OF A FISHING BOAT

Lurching to-and-fro
prow dissects grey ocean waves
lifts bubbling white foam
rises cool salty fragrance
as if from some sea flower

Saturday's Second Catch

A fishing boat idles then stops over a rolling blue-green bed of floating seaweed. They drop lines with wriggling salt smelling anchovies as bait and watch and wait. A massive lingcod thrashes furiously on the end. This fisherman leans back, strains calves and sweats to reel it up through the broken water's surface. The whistling high noon wind kicks up chopping slate waves.

 porpoise rises
breaks the line—sweeps cod for lunch
while man frowns a boy laughs

CHAIN OF TEARS

Tears of salt
salt of sea
sea of mist
mist of clouds
clouds of rain
rain of water
water of wine
wine of sacrament
sacrament of sacrifice
sacrifice of love
love of Christ
Christ of Gethsemane
Gethsemane of liberty
liberty of soul
soul of joy
joy of tears
tears of salt

113   An Inclination to Believe

In the eroding rocky landscape of super-skeptic rationality
some people will mock any leaning to believe.

Disbelieving everything out of hand may lead
to a chair at the banquet of self-superiority,
but at the end of the day, when you believe nothing
of anything
      is there not a void of meaning
            and a high cost to pay?

Others may choose their roads, but I will start with an inclina-
tion to believe.
It activates and enlivens the senses to further observation and
inquiry,
opens reasoning from a multitude of vista points previously
unconceived
and empowers me to kneel at the throne to receive inspiration
from Deity.

When observation, inquiry, reasoning and inspiration meld
my belief and faith will slough away
leaving the godly alloy of knowledge and truth
to stand with in that

Great Last Day.

An observation, my friend.
You seem to want
to drive, white-knuckled,
the big yellow bus
of all eternal
existences by yourself,
with half a mortal life
of experience,
instead of letting
God do
all-knowing wonders
everywhere and for everyone.

No wonder you appear
so weary and stressed,
not knowing
what is just around
the next hairpin curve.

Come, let's sit
for a while
in the coolness
of the Garden, rest
easy in Me,
my Precious Child.
Buses can wait.

www.ingramcontent.com/pod-product-compliance
Lightning Source LLC
Chambersburg PA
CBHW052006090426
42741CB00008B/1571